Let Faith Do It!

Dr. Michelle Fields

Kingdom Kaught Publishing
Denton, Maryland 21629
www.kingdomkaughtpublishing.com

Let Faith Do It!
Dr. Michelle Fields

Copyright © 2013 by Dr. Michelle Fields

All rights reserved.

No part of this book may be reproduced or transmitted in any form or by any means without written permission of the author.

All scripture is taken from the King James Version of the Holy Bible unless otherwise noted.

ISBN 978-0-9824550-6-7

LCCN Number: 2011940580

Cover design by *Agape Advertisement, Inc.*

This book is dedicated to the Mothers of the Faith who taught us how to pray, how to trust God and how to believe in His Word. To the Women of God who dared to stand on the promises of God in the face of adversity so they could stand on Sunday morning and testify of the goodness of the Lord, that we may believe and receive strength. And to all of the young upcoming Sister Believers who will have all of our shoulders to stand on as they face their journey.

Acknowledgments

I would like to take a moment to give thanks first to God for granting me the ability to share this message through the overcoming power of Jesus Christ and the creative power of Holy Spirit who led me and directed me in the truth.

To my family and friends for their support and encouragement.

To my husband, Pastor Vincent E. Fields, Sr., who has been a confidant and contributor many times not even knowing, by his awesome godly insight and scriptural knowledge.

To our daughter Terese, being the first one to read the book in rough draft, whose review was... and I quote ....."I felt like shouting when I read that book!" To Kelli our oldest daughter who has always been a faithful supporter and Vince Jr. who is writing a powerful testimonial right now.

To Bishop Herbert James for referring me to Kingdom Kaught Publishing.

To Bishop Antonio Palmer and Kingdom Kaught Publishing, LLC, for their expertise and patience in helping me to deliver this manuscript.

To Bishop Jerry Grillo, Jr. for writing that powerful forward and his willingness to support kingdom effort.

To every Pastor who has ever imparted into my life... that which has brought me to the kingdom mindset that I obtain today.

Foreword

When I think of someone whose life has been a living testimony, I think of Michelle Fields. I have known Michelle and her husband for many years.

I have witnessed them go through battles, encounter scars and pain, but come out victorious! They are an example of what God expects from His children to exit seasons of struggle and enter seasons of success.

Information is costly. Truth never comes free. Someone always has to pay a price in order to mentor others for growth and change. Michelle has paid that price. Her anointing and wisdom didn't come cheap. Years of experience have given birth to this book you hold in your hands today.

I believe that God has anointed Michelle as one of His mouthpieces for the last days. The information written within the pages of this book can help propel you into your next season. Use this book as a part of your daily devotion; read it alongside of God's word. Watch your life experience increase and prosper.

Dr. Jerry A Grillo, Jr.
The Favor Center Church
Hickory, North Carolina

Table of Contents

Dedication

Acknowledgements

Foreword

Introduction 1

Chapter 1 3

The Operation of Faith/Surrogate Faith 3

Chapter 2 7

"The Attendant" - Attentive Faith 7

Chapter 3 11

Praise Him Anyhow 11

Chapter 4 15

Because He Told Me – "STAND" 15

Chapter 5 21

Obedient "Submission" Faith 21

Chapter 6 23

Faith through the Prophetic 23

Chapter 7 27

The Power of Declaration and Decrees 27

"Speak It by Faith" 27

Chapter 8 33

The Cost of Disobedience 33
"Faith for Foolishness" 33
Chapter 9 39
The Thing I Feared the Most Has Come Upon Me 39
Chapter 10 47
Align Your Faith.. 47
"A Faith Alignment" 47
Chapter 11 51
So Very God!.. 51

Introduction

    This book is a written compilation of the many testimonies that I have acquired over my years of walking with the Lord. It testifies of the goodness of the Lord in the land of the living and of His faithfulness, mercy and gracious response to His Word to those who will dare to believe and activate the principles thereof. The variations of the application of "Faith" will express how I obtained victorious results by simply believing God's Word and acting on what I believed to be truth. Remember, it is the truth that you know that makes you free. You must believe that what God says is truth. Even though you may be confronted with specific facts, you must then engage in and activate the word by being a "doer" of the word, mixing it with faith and then support those efforts by speaking the word in order to get results. These kingdom principles are guaranteed to produce results because God said so, now how simple is that?

    "In the beginning was the Word," as John 1:1 tells us, "and the Word was with God and the Word was God." Verse 2 states, "The same was in the beginning with God." John here speaks of the eternal Christ, the WORD or the "LOGOS," His existence and how He, after conferring with and originating everything according to the Divine Council, becomes the Word Himself - "The Divine Expression" of the spoken thought of God. Because the Word is the spoken thought of God, and because He cannot be separated from Himself, He is not apart from His Word. Therefore, if we can believe in God, we should have no problem believing His Word. Words are powerful. Even the spoken word of a human being has jurisdictional power in the elements. So if a judge can speak and it happen at his word, how much more can the Word of Almighty God, the "Super Judge" have preeminence over and superseded anything in the earth? Words can build, destroy or create, sink ships and have the power of life and death in them. God spoke "words" and the world's existence began (Heb. 11:3). We have the ability to use the word of the Lord and obtain tangible results from the supernatural realm that will eventually manifest in the natural realm.

Jesus being fashioned after many O.T. patterns is an expression of the love that God had for His people and His desire to deliver them. So again, before we can come to God we must first believe that He is (Heb.11:6), and if we ask anything in His name (I John 5: 14-15), and if this is the confidence that we have in Him.(v. 15), and if we can speak to the mountain and it be removed (Matt. 17:20) *AND* if we have faith as a grain of mustard seed then we can receive the manifestation of the Word of God in our lives without fail.

Chapter 1

The Operation of Faith/Surrogate Faith

One of my very first experiences with the "operation" of Faith and having to stand on the Word of God was in a time when I, a newly baptized believer, didn't even understand much of what was required of one who had to believe beyond the visible. After returning from Bermuda (back in my B. C days), I met a young lady who was locked into an apartment lease but wanted to return to her hometown. We made an agreement and I took over the apartment, however, when it was time to renew the lease I was challenged. Because my name was not on the lease and the young lady was not able to return in ample time to complete the transfer as we planned to do, I was considered to be a "squatter" by the management office and they asked me to produce certain documentation or prepare to remove my belongings from the premises. After considering the "facts", I decided to pack my bags. With tears in my eyes and feeling defeated, suddenly a knock came at the door. It was my grandmother, Amanda Queen Esther "Honeymoon" Dixon! (I think my mom said someone nicknamed her "Honeymoon" because "The Honeymooners" was one of her favorite shows). She enters with these words as she stood firm and walked in authority and assurance, "Don't pack another box! You and that baby are not moving anywhere; you have to have faith in God!" I heard her, but what I heard wasn't very clear because I had the letter that spelled it all out and it was on the official letterhead from the company with a signature of the person who was in authority to make it happen! However, my grandmother proclaimed, "I have made arrangements for you to talk to a lawyer and don't pack anything else!"

Who doesn't believe or obey gra'ma though? She's the one person who most likely for many of us, is that one person who knows God and trusts Him at another level. The one whose life you've had a chance to observe, as she served God year after year with joy, God making many ways for her and answering many prayers. Thank God for grandmom's faith! That is surrogate faith, relying upon the faith of another. When we can't see a way, thank God that there is someone who trusts God at His word enough and has favor with Him to help us believe and obtain the victory over our circumstance and to gain vision. Someone we can attach our hope to until we learn "Faith" and until we are able to stand on our own.

Sure enough, I met with the lawyer who represented me on the day of court. She was planning to make a deal or at least buy some time. On the day of court, both representing lawyers met outside of the courtroom to discuss the case and try to come to a reasonable agreement. Whatever they discussed didn't seem favorable for me or agreeable to the manager representing the rental property. "We're going before the judge" said my lawyer, "You sit out here for now and let us go before the judge and I will come get you when it's time." I sat praying of course. Oh, did I mention that I was about 7 or 8 months pregnant with my second child? I believe at this time, not knowing what to expect, yet open to witness the work of God and trying to understand faith at this level; one has anticipation but maybe not expectation. I guess it was no more than a half an hour later when my lawyer came suddenly bursting around the corner in excitement. "You won! You won! The

The Operation of Faith/Surrogate Faith

judge ruled in your favor! The whole case has turned around! The judge said, 'because you paid rent in your name (for about 8 months) and because they received it willingly is indicative of them making an agreement to do business with you and that your rent was honored as you being a resident.' They should have never taken your money and now the judge said you are taking them to court! The judge wants to know what you want to do?" By this time, my mouth of course was wide open. Talk about not knowing the law! I witnessed God turn things around in my favor by using the faith of my grandmother. Of course, I opted to arrange for a lease agreement and resolve our housing issue. I eventually lived on that property way past the rental manager's employment and was offered a 3-bedroom apartment by the new manager a few years later. It was there that I established my evangelistic ministry called, "Project Redemption," ministering to many people and gathering the youth in the community, teaching them scriptures, songs, how to sew, and also providing activities, snacks, coordinating "street meetings," Christian rappers and some of the areas greatest witnesses, and age-related ministers. We had deliverance meetings, where people were having demons cast out of them and being baptized with the Holy Ghost and making decisions for Christ. It was there that all of my children were baptized and filled with the Holy Spirit. I remember on one occasion when a Jehovah's Witness student knocked on the door during one of their Saturday witnessing routines in the neighborhood. Needless to say, he left my porch saved, confessing Jesus as his Savior. He seemed a little confused as to how it all happened but a new recipient of the salvation plan. It was there that I learned to fast and pray and lay before God and seek His face. Children in the neighborhood were being

Let Faith Do It!

trained in the things of God, walking around the neighborhood singing the "get free from drugs song" while parents peeped out of the windows in conviction. No wonder the enemy wanted me out of there. He evidently saw what was coming!

Chapter 2

"The Attendant" - Attentive Faith

Proverbs 4:20-22
"20) My son, give attention to my words, incline your ear to my sayings. 21) Do not let them depart from your eyes: Keep them in the midst of your heart; 22) For they are life to those who find them, and health to all their flesh."

Even though the enemy and his relentless tactics give opportunity for us to grow in faith, I'm sure the consensus is that we would rather take a written exam or just have God trust that we believe Him without the tests that come to try our faith. 1 Peter 4:12 is one of those scriptures that help us to make sense of things when the fiery trials come because it teaches us not to think that these things that happen to us are strange but to rejoice because we share in Christ's sufferings and when His glory comes we will be glad with exceeding joy also. At first that's not so easy to do, but as we encounter more tests it becomes easier to trust God, because our confidence in God is increased as He proves Himself in each test and we get the "bring-it-on-Mr.-Devil!" attitude, because we just know our God will not fail us. The greatest weapon that we have in our arsenal is the WORD of GOD - the quick and powerful sword that pierces and divides asunder! It is this powerful weapon that the enemy must come subject to. I said "MUST" come subject to and obey the living Word! And it will accomplish exactly what God sends it to. Satan does not have authority over God's Word. Remember? He is already defeated by it! It is that great sword (of the Spirit) found in Ephesians chapter 6, which is our offensive and defensive weapon.

While listening to a Gloria Copeland message on healing and applying Proverbs 4:20 as a prescription (as was instructed), it just made sense to me to read the healing scriptures and digest them every so many hours just like I would medicine, like when I was diagnosed with having a fibroid tumor. It's something about getting the Word of God deep in your heart, making it a part of your very fiber. David said, *"Thy word have I hid in my heart that I might not sin against thee"* (Ps.119:11). The Word that can cut anything will cut the devil's every plan, plot, scheme and endeavor! Studies show that if you repeat something five times, after the fifth time, it sinks in and you really believe what you say. Well, all I can tell you is… one late afternoon, while at home, I needed to use the bathroom before going to church. I was attending Full Gospel Deliverance under the leadership of Pastors Charles and Patricia Miller. It was a very powerful apostolic ministry with signs and wonders following the Word. People healed from incurable diseases, brought back from the dead, and fear was stripped from the words cancer and AIDS. It was a prophetic, teaching ministry with anointed praise and worship. All night shut-ins and prayer warriors who loved to war (you remember?). So after using the bathroom, as I turned to flush, I noticed something floating in the commode that looked a little abnormal, so I looked a little closer to see what in the world?…I couldn't believe what I was seeing. There it was… the fibroid tumor! By the Word of God that tumor was out! Of course I had to examine it. It was a round, fleshy matter, ugly and evident that it had a form.

How demonic I thought! It appeared to be throbbing as if it had life.

That night, when I got to the church (that's a good place to scream) - we were having a revival & our guest preacher was Prophetess Helena Bynum - I gave my testimony. Prophetess Bynum was quickened in the Spirit (you know saints used to 'get quickened' as we called it). Oh the power of consecration and abiding in the presence of the Lord via fasting and prayer meetings! Anyway, she stood up and said as I was testifying that the Holy Ghost showed her the tumor falling in the commode. Oh, I bless His name! I learned that you have to *attend* to the Word. Attend is defined as "attention like babysitting." Good instruction: read the word and apply it just like you would a prescription from the doctor. Good medicine, the Word of God (Proverbs 3:8 is health to your navel and healing for your soul and 2 Samuel 22:31 *"as for God, His way is perfect, the Word of the Lord is tried; He is a buckler to all them that trust Him"*). *"But unto you that fear my name shall the Sun of righteousness arise with healing in his wings"* (Malachi 4:2a).

Chapter 3

Praise Him Anyhow

Because Faith is the substance of things hoped for and the evidence of things not seen, (Hebrews 11:1), *Praise Him Anyhow!*

One of my next encounters that granted me the opportunity to experience the power of God's Word was in the early 1990's. I've heard it called an advanced praise or a praise in advance because "God's credit is good." It's your anyhow praise or some call it a "High praise from a low place." Just right in the devil's face, praise God! Justa' "whose report will you believe" praise! Nevertheless, in my studying, I also found out that it's called *"paltazok"* which is the Hebrew word for *a praise attack on the enemy, a break out or sudden praise.* My family is known for the Praise Attack. For years, a practice of ours has been that at any time, with everyone at home involved in their own activities, at the given command, "PRAISE ATTACK!" We would all stop what we're doing all over the house and just start praising God as an attack against the enemy.

One time, during a routine follow up, after receiving an annual mammogram some weeks prior, the doctor entered the room, took a seat, unveiled the x-rays and told me that he regretted to inform me that the test showed a lump in one of my breast. You know the attack of the enemy comes without advance notice. That's why we have to "stay prayed up." Now that's an old term that is still relevant. He then gave me further instructions and told me he needed to see me back in the office within a certain time frame for a return visit and then he just left the office. At that moment, alone in a cold examination room with no pastor, prayer partner or Hammond organ, with the enemy trying his hardest to force and re-enforce that negative report *and* plant fear in my mind, I began to think on the Word of God and my immediate responsive weapon for that season and situation was "praise." Not knowing what else to do with the information that came so suddenly and so unexpectedly, I felt a need to respond immediately to protect my spirit and to disallow the enemy from accessing my immediate thoughts. I didn't even give the 'soul man' any time to begin to even think of receiving any of those words. We must remember that we are tri-part beings: Spirit, Soul and Body and one part is going to rule, based upon appetite and diet. If you constantly kill the flesh, the spirit man will be the stronger, vice versa. If you constantly feed the flesh, the spirit man will be the weaker and the enemy fights in the soulish realm. There are also three definitions of man: 1) the Natural man is the *"psychikos"* (1 Corinthians 2:14). He operates in his Adamic nature and receives not the things of God. This is an unregenerate being; 2) the Spiritual man *"pneumatikos"* is the man who in 1 Corinthians 2:15 walks with God according to His word and judges things and 3) is the Carnal or "fleshly" man, *"sarkikos"* (1 Corinthians 3:1), who has been regenerated but yields to the flesh (just thought I'd throw that in for ya'). I spontaneously leaped up off of the exam table and began to dance and utter in a silent but projected voice, "Hallelujah! Hallelujah!" You know - that under-your-breath-but-serious praise. It's kind of like when you get the job but don't want the employer to know how elated you are so you remain calm on the outside, but all on the inside you're snapping! So there I am, all alone in my moment, yet not alone because the Comforter who abides with us always, was right there with me in that moment of time and we began to dance. I was making sure that I was targeting the negative words spoken over me and also making sure that I was clear in my declaration that this dance was to let the enemy know that I didn't receive what was said and that I was praising on a promise and claiming the victory and rejoicing because I had a report far above his and I was going to praise Him anyhow! In the face of adversity and uncertainty, I was relying on His Word!

Now you might say, "How does anyone win a war by dancing?" My answer to you would then be, "David, the man who is our example of one who pleased God and worshipped Him as he danced out of his garment." Dancing makes a bold and declarative statement that you would rather bask in the fullness of joy in the presence of God than to submit to sadness and gloom. Dancing and praising are an expression of celebration. Psalms 150:4 also commands us to praise Him in a dance. Now we know that our God is a God of purpose and any command that He gives is a well thought out, strategic plan that will result in supernatural and relative outcomes. Psalms 30:11 says, *"He turns our mourning into dancing and girded me with gladness."* Many times in scripture, we see the Israelites dancing after the great spoil. But when you can dance BEFORE He brings you out, before the slaughter of the Philistines...that's faith! When you praise God in advance, it informs the devil that you still trust God and still believe that He is a man of His word and it shows God that you are celebrating His intervention. The Hebrew Boys put it like this, (if I may paraphrase) "Even if He doesn't do it, we know that He can, so keep living, oh King!"

Let Faith Do It!

The end result: I returned to the follow-up appointment to get the final result of the x-rays. The doctor said, "I don't know what happened but the lump is gone." Yup! That's a good place to praise Him, right there, right there! Our faithful God! who is always teaching us, building our faith and introducing Himself in new ways, showed up just like His word said He would!

Now would I tell you to dance if the doctor gives you a negative report? I would say stand on the Word of God but I would also say that God gives different strategies at different times of war. Be open to what He tells you to do, always mixing the Word with faith, being a *"doer"* of the Word. Faith must be put to action. Being inspired to dance at that time was an act of faith as I knew faith to be in that season of my life and praise is always a weapon and it does still the enemy. 1 Chronicles 20:21 says, *"And when he had consulted of the people, he appointed singers unto the Lord and that should praise the beauty of holiness, as they went out before the army and to say, Praise the Lord for His mercy endureth forever 22: and when they began to sing and to praise, the Lord set ambushments against the children of Ammon, Moab, and Mt. Seir, which were come against Judah (praise) and they were smitten.* The enemy will come against your praise also. So when you find yourself lacking in praise and do a self 'oil check" and realize you haven't been or don't feel like praising - Paltazok! Just stop what you're doing and initiate a praise attack! You'll feel much better after you do. We are encouraged to "put on the garment of praise." New Testament confirmation: Rm. 15:13, Heb. 13:15, Is. 61:3, Ps. 3, and Ps. 8.

Put on the garment of PRAISE!

Chapter 4

Because He Told Me – *"STAND"*

Joseph dreamed a dream and in spite of what his brothers said or how they responded to his revelation of the plan of God for his future, he had to stand on what he believed to be God inspired. There will be times in our walk in Christendom that we will have to stand on what we believe that we know-that-we-know, that-we-know, by the Spirit of God via faith. Our faith for the vision has to supersede the critics, doubters, haters, scoffers, forecasters of doom, the familiar spirits, customs, traditions of men, the faithless, the complacent, the legalist, the heretics and whosoever or what-so-ever the enemy will send to discount what God has said to you. We must keep on believing God regardless! We must not be moved, because without faith it is impossible to please God (Heb.11:6). What do you do? STAND and WITHSTAND. According to Ephesians 6:13-14, we are told to stand and after we have done all that we can do to stand, we are told to stand some more and to withstand in the evil day. Well it is possible to be pushed over while just standing in one position, but once one withstands, braced with feet planted strongly in front of them with shoulders firm, one is not so easily moved.

Many times, we expect others to see our vision as clearly as we do and the truth is that God has not given others the ability to see it as He has shown it to us at that time. Oftentimes shepherds have to reiterate the vision over and over until the people catch on. Fortunate is the leader who has parishioners who catch the vision quickly and run with it. We also need to know that everything God reveals to us isn't necessarily meant to be released until specific times. Sometimes God is sharing secrets with His trusted. Sometimes He shows us things to pray about and sometimes He is showing us things to begin to prepare for. He expands our hope for greater things and reveals His potential to do in us what we know will definitely have to be His working. It is unfair to demand that others see the vision as clearly as you do. Everyone doesn't have the capacity to operate in the realm of the invisible. Some may be still growing also and 1 Corinthians 13:12 tell us that we do see in part.

    Moses was handpicked by God for a specific task and God spoke with him pertaining to the assignment that included people. We need to remember that in God's business of leading people, there will be some who will operate in general revelation and some will be able to see beyond the natural. If every believer had the ability to see otherwise, they would not have need of a shepherd. In all honesty, with a genuine spirit of humility and in pure love, we sometimes share that which needs to stay tucked away until an appointed time and regarded as sacred. Just thought I'd throw that in.

    So, the 3rd encounter is when I was asked by a dear sister in the Lord to accompany her one day to the hospital to visit a co-worker's sister to pray for her. I agreed and off we went. I didn't know the lady we were going to pray for, so I cannot attribute anything that happened to my relationship, spiritual connection or anything like that but what I was getting ready to witness would supernaturally charge my faith and increase my confidence in God to a whole 'nother level. (I know 'nother). As we entered the ICU hospital room, I noticed the tubes that were taped to her mouth and facial area and as we walked in closer, I noticed the tremendous swelling in her body. She was apparently unconscious, laying there appearing unaware of her surroundings or what was going on in her life and what I was seeing was the evidence of something more than what I expected to see on a week day afternoon lunch break.

The family had been called in from near and far, which is customary when the doctor's determine that there is nothing else that can be done by medical science. A few of the family members entered and exited the room, viewing her body and making small comments as some were seated in the waiting area. I remember one family member's statement in particular "She looks just like mama looked when she died too." Apparently, the doctors stated that this was the worst case of leukemia that they had seen. We positioned ourselves around the patient's bed, one of us on each side while my dear sister in the Lord opens her pocketbook to take out her bottle of anointing oil. I've always known her to be serious about the work of God, never operating in timidity or hesitation at anytime. She was and still is a woman of God who is about God's business. I was confident that she was in total control of the situation. As we began to pour the oil in our hands, preparing to lay hands on the lady, I guess out of respect for our prayer assignment, the last family member excused herself from the room.

This is where it all begins. We're standing over the body, split seconds away from laying hands and suddenly, I hear a small still voice say, "Close the door." I cannot move because this may very well be the first time I'm hearing the audible voice of God! I inwardly suggested to God, "Here's this lady that I don't even know and she's at death's door and you decide to give me a voice training?"

Let Faith Do It!

God's timing is amazing. I've never encountered anything like this but I'm a believer, Lord I want to believe! Again I hear "close the door" and now I'm looking around the room for like…what…? Confirmation? Or oh…. maybe I'm trying not to disturb the atmosphere. Yeah right, I was scared! Right then a nurse walks by the room, turns around, comes back and mysteriously closes the door, out of nowhere for no reason. My goodness, how powerful is that! "Whew! Thank you Lord." Isn't it amazing how suspended time (which seems like forever) is really only a few moments? That is why God is not bound by time and there is no distance in prayer and we cannot put a time limit on when we think God should move in the Spirit. He does not work by clock time *"Chronos."* He works by *"Kairos,"* a fixed season (more about that later). So now, door closed and we begin to pray when suddenly I hear another message, "I'm going to heal her." With that, I get excited and share the news with my dear sister, whispering the first time. "God said He's going to heal her, He's going to heal her! I began to decree, then louder… He's going to heal her! Faith time! Let's get moving with the Spirit! Excitedly, I began laying hands everywhere; on her, on the beeping machines, on everything in the room, you name it (I was young). "He's going to do it! He said it!" Well, since He told me and I had no better sense than to believe it. What else at this point? Hope is all that's left so let's fuel it with some faith. Why do I believe it? Because He said so! So often God has spoken things to us and if we are not careful, we will allow the opinions of others or either their dogmatic unbelief or lack of understanding has swayed us away from what God has said. We must stand on what God has spoken to us and make no excuse about it!

After our prayer, with some of the family members still proclaiming her hopeless based upon what the doctors said and what it looked like in the room, I realized that my sister too was concerned that the lady didn't look like she was going to make it and yes, as believers we have sometimes prayed for people and they have not been healed. Our responsibility, however, is to pray the prayer of faith and not to respond to what things look like. Faith is not faith if you can see it. This is what we did as we agreed in faith, remember? In all fairness, if I'm the one who God spoke to, it's not fair to expect others to walk in that revelation if they haven't received it. So be careful not to judge people who do not see as you see. You just keep standing on what God said. Someone's very life could be depending upon it.

Well, the report is that the next day, she opened her eyes. The day after that, she sat up, followed by the removing of the tubes and eating to feeding herself to and ultimately being released and sent home healed! We serve an amazing God! That was well over 20 years ago.

Chapter 5

Obedient "Submission" Faith

Now this one was enlightening. I had heard it preached and heard testimonies of things like this happening, and I believed its possibilities because I knew God was able to do anything. Hearing the audible voice of God was something that I was now being trained to hear and recognize. Today the Holy Spirit leads and guides us into all truths and speaks as the third person of the Godhead. Many times people do not hear the audible voice of God but receive a knowing in their spirit or He speaks to them in various other ways, like through reading the word, or in dreams, or through other people such as prophetic gifts or your leader in the Sunday morning message, to name a few. But by now, I have enough sense to know His voice as stated in the book of John, "my sheep know my voice and a stranger they will not follow" (John 10:27).

So, I'm home one day watching '_able (selah). That is whatever I am *able* to get on the television because the cable was disconnected and I heard His sweet voice say "Call the Cable Company and have your service connected." Of course we have to challenge and try everything that we hear when it doesn't make sense. When the flesh talks or the devil is speaking relative to our fleshly desire, oh how easy it is to jump right away and be so sorrowful, pitiful and regretful after we get the end results, on many occasions. Not to say that it isn't good to try the spirits, we need to know what voices are speaking, because there are many voices in the land. Let me rephrase that; we better

Let Faith Do It!

know what voice is speaking! I'll have to tell you about that one too! Oh I'm not going to tell you about all of the good results and leave out the times I didn't listen, and suffered the consequences, because faith comes by hearing and we can obtain faith for some foolishness also.

Nevertheless, I had this conversation with God about how I owe the company money and how they will know *if* I call and yada, yada. Again, I hear, clearly, "Call the Cable Company." So I call. "Alright Lord, but you know what they're going to say." Nevertheless, I dialed, they answered, I gave them my request, they asked my name (I'm almost whispering it through a stutter), they look in the system, said "o.k.," gave me a date for service installation and proceeded with the order. I said, "Um, Miss, do you see a previous bill or a balance?" "No ma'am, I don't see anything in here with your name on it" was her response. "So let me spell it for you miss" (I say like, well, enough isn't good enough). "No miss, I don't see anything here in the negative for you!" Daddy God had done it again! He increased my faith and took me to another understanding of how things work in the faith realm in His kingdom. Sometimes, He just wants to be daddy and bless us and our *obedience* is key. This answered the question I had about some of the testimonies I heard from the saints of how God can get in the computer and erase their debts. God can do anything! He owns it all! How many need Him to get in the computer right now? I know that's right!

Chapter 6

Faith through the Prophetic

In 2 Chronicles 20:20, Jehoshaphat is instructed to believe God's prophets and prosper. The first part of the text says to believe in the Lord your God and you shall be established.

Jesus says for the believers that it is given unto us to know the mysteries of this age, and God reveals His secrets to His prophets (Matthews 13:11 & Luke 8: 10). We are now living in what is called, "The Information Age," where so many things are revealed, i.e. it is a revelation era for all, general knowledge as well as the spiritual mysteries of Christ, because nothing is hidden anymore. You can find anything you need to know on the worldwide web, information highway, Google, Wikipedia, Ask.com and more.

Prophetic Ministry was proclaimed for this time by the Prophet Joel, *"For in the last days I will pour out my spirit on all flesh, your sons and daughters shall prophesy, old men shall see dreams and young men shall see visions"* (Joel 2:28). God is confirming His Word in this hour as the prophetic and the apostolic anointing are prevalent in the body of Christ. Jesus is the spirit of prophecy! The gifts are in operation in the Spirit-filled, bible-based assembly and there is an outpouring on the hungry, the Godchasers, the diligent seekers and those who believe like Mark 16. The believers are becoming more and more empowered with the clearly interpreted Word in this hour because of the available information. And they are walking into dimensions with greater levels of comprehension of the operation of the gifts. Some, God has called to the "Office" of Prophet, as explained in Ephesians 4. This is one of the five-fold gifts, as others, Holy Spirit may choose to use at a specific time to relay a message according to the nine operational gifts of the Spirit, by way of 1) Word of Wisdom, 2) Word of Knowledge or 3) Prophesy.

On a few occasions I can remember God by supernatural intervention, using my very children to speak to me and encourage me in the faith. Once, upon receiving a very bad letter of discouragement, I guess I must have spoken out loud my concern and my little son, "Tuffy" (as we call him) no more than 3 to 4 years at that time, said "Come on mommy, let's dance on it!" I replied, "Ok" and placed the letter on the floor. To my amazement, he grabbed both of my hands and began to circle as if in 'ring around the rosy'. I could feel the anointing, knowing that he did not have this kind of strength as a young child to twirl me around. Later I learned that 'circling' was a prophetic act of a spiritual warfare tactic to protect the subject by setting up a hedge around it. This stops the enemy from gaining access to the subject. Needless to say, I was victorious over the matter and I never forgot what the Lord had done that evening nor how He used my Spirit-filled son in prophetic demonstration.

The next one I remember is when I was sitting in my bedroom feeling forsaken, as we sometimes do during times of hard trials, despondent at heart like David in Psalms 42:5, *"Why art thou cast down, O my soul and why art thou disquieted within me?"* All of a sudden, out of nowhere, my second and youngest daughter came in the bedroom and began to sing an old hymn that children her age (probably 5 or 6 years of age), don't even know. By this act, God knew He had my undivided attention and my faith was immediately increased and I joined in with her and began to sing the song, with a reminder that "We have come this far by faith, leaning on the Lord." I immediately put on a garment of praise for the spirit of heaviness (Isaiah 61:3). God often used her in this manner.

Again, I remember my oldest daughter, coming to me saying, "Mommy I feel sick." Being parents, sometimes our emotions get in the way when matters are close and personal. I was an evangelist at this time and knew the Word, signs following and answered prayers. I felt her head with my hand, went to the cabinet, pulled out the thermometer, took her temperature, read it and immediately went back to the cabinet to get the necessary medication. I had it all together and she looked up at me about 12 years of age or so and said, "All of this and you haven't prayed for me yet." Talk about a rebuke! And I knew better! How embarrassing to have your very own child rebuke you for not operating in James 5:14-15, "Is any among you sick, let him call for the elders of the church and they..." We have to be very careful how we handle the gospel especially in our homes and amongst those the closest to us because our loved ones are in observation. If they are not reading the book, they are reading you. My reply was, "You know what, you're right." Then I prayed. I am not telling you to not use medicine, but I am telling you to pray first. Give God a chance to be the first responder. We sometimes run with the doctor's prescription without even adding God to the equation. All of our children were Spirit-filled at an early age: ages 7, 4 and 3 ½. This same child spoke a word based upon a "Toys R Us" commercial one day which eventually inspired one of the greatest youth messages I'd ever preached. Prayer works!

Sometimes, we disregard the thoughts and conversations of our children thinking children should be seen and not heard and counting them as menial. Where is that written? Besides, if your children are Spirit-filled, why can't God use them? Not only that, but if God used a donkey, He can use anybody! In the book of Matthews, Jesus rebuked the disciples and told them not to stop the children but to let the children come to Him. He also said we had to have the heart of the children for of such belongs the kingdom of heaven Ever turn on the television and hear someone speaking directly to you? Ever hear people that you don't even know, in a grocery store or somewhere, talking and suddenly Holy Ghost zooms you in on their conversation and you realize that God positioned you near them just to use them to speak to you?

Chapter 7

The Power of Declaration and Decrees
"Speak It by Faith"

Upon attending a Morris Cerrillo Conference one year with some of my Christian sisters, R. W. Shambach, being one of the keynote speakers and of course, being "RW", a great man of faith, taught on the "Foolishness of the Gospel." I'll never forget it. In his message, he expounded on those scriptures in the New Testament where Jesus performed some of the most profound acts of healing and deliverance during His ministry on earth that appeared to be foolish actions but demonstrated the power of God. Spitting in the mud and healing the blind man, Peter walking on water at Jesus' bid to come, speaking to fig trees, rocks prepared to cry out, raising the dead and all of the stories that we've grown accustomed to appreciate that teach and equip us as believers to operate in the same faith. "RW's" emphasis was on the power to speak and to decree and declare God's word and obtain results. Proverbs 18:21 tells us that life and death are in the power of the tongue and the book of James (3:8) teaches us about the tongue's power to sink ships if it is not bridled.

For me this was just what I needed, the power to decree a thing and to walk in expectation, while watching for the manifestation. Calling those things that be not as though they were. You see, my car had just been stolen some weeks ago and the police just couldn't seem to catch the culprit. Amazing, how I could be walking home in the rain after work one day, just picking up my children from

Let Faith Do It!

After School programs and the babysitter and I can see my car pass by about 3 blocks across the road, right before my eyes but the police couldn't find my car in the little town of Atlantic City with all of their forces, for weeks! Nevertheless, I'm sure they had bigger fish to fry and criminals to catch, and because this was a spiritual battle, it was going to take a God encounter to resolve it. How my car was stolen in the first place was when a person of another religious belief that a co-worker and I were ministering to, made a vow that if we prayed for him and if the lump in his chest went away, he'd come to church. Well, we prayed and the lump went away so it wasn't strange when he knocked on my door one Sunday morning asking for a ride to church. Excited about what God had done (naïve), I introduced him to my pastor who was in the neighborhood picking up people for Sunday School, in the church van and off we all went. For some strange reason when we stopped for the "Sunday morning store run," (he riding with me and my family), my car didn't start when I got back in, i.e. pastor took me to church on the van and went back with him to see what the problem was with the car, then, once done, the co-worker was to drive it to the church. "Wham!" Car gone.

Yup! This was just what I needed to hear, as a person growing in faith and learning how to use faith for circumstances beyond my control. I was getting ready to try just what RW said. Speak it and decree it and watch it come to past. But speak it with the authority that Jesus gave you to use. Once I returned home from the conference, I stood in the middle of my bedroom floor and spoke to my car (stolen for about three weeks by now) and said something like this: "Car! You belong to me, God gave you to me and you don't have any business driving no criminals around. You get somewhere where the police can see you and bring yourself home!" With that, I turned off the light and went to bed. About 1:00 a.m. that morning, the phone rang. You know we don't like the phone to ring early in the morning, it startles us. To my surprise, it was a Philadelphia police officer. "Yes," I said after answering the phone and the officer acknowledging who he was. "Ma'am, are you the owner of a yellow Dodge Aries K-Car? (Young folks, that's before your time)." "Yes," I replied. He said "Well ma'am, I believe you reported your vehicle stolen and we are in possession of your vehicle and the perpetrator has been apprehended." He told me the location where I could pick up the car and all of the information I needed regarding it. My mouth is wide open, I mean w-i-d-e open as he is talking and I am sitting up now, looking up to heaven shaking my head in astonishment, with mixed emotions. We don't know who we are in Christ. Why don't we know this and how do we not operate in this everyday for every need? How awesome is this! Before we hung up, I stopped the officer and asked "Sir, sir, just one thing, how did you find the car?" He said, "One of our officers stopped the car on a routine check because one of the tail lights was out." Now, I don't know about you, but how simple was that!

Sometimes we give into circumstances and illnesses because we don't know how to exercise our faith and speak the Word of God using it as the two-edged sword that it is. *"The Word is a hammer that breaketh the rock in pieces!"* (Jeremiah 23:29). We have power that we have not tapped into in many instances, because of traditions, religion, lack of knowledge, forms of godliness, misinterpretation/misrepresentation of the Word, fear, and timidity. Because of this, we don't obtain victory, and we lack the

Let Faith Do It!

dunamis power God gave us. Healing belongs to us! James reminds us that as believers, we have a right to be healed, even if we have sinned, the prayer of faith prayed by the elders will cause our sins to be forgiven. How awesome is that?

So, one day I felt some kind of virus coming on. I use to say, "I'm catching a cold" and "I think I'm coming down with something," but now I don't confess those things nor do I offer access to spirits of infirmity to trespass on God's holy ground in His temple where His Holy Spirit resides by speaking things with my mouth contrary to the Word. I just simply keep my words aligned with what God has said already, regardless of the situation. We cannot be moved! Sometimes we open ourselves up to things because of what we confess and profess out of our mouths. It's amazing how many bible professing Christians make statements like "I was dying laughing" and "My diabetes" and "I'm so broke," and "I think I'm going to be sick." I remember one time a sister called the church on like a Friday to say she wasn't going to be in church on Sunday because she thought she was going to be sick. We appreciated her diligence in preparing us for her absence but it just seemed like the jury was still out on the verdict. God still had a chance to intervene and change the circumstance. Even Nyquil can work in two days.

Yes, fact is fact but truth is truth. Read Isaiah 53. Fact is, I feel something trying to attach itself to me, and we do live in this flesh, but truth is, "By His stripes I am healed!" regardless of the facts. Whose report will you believe? Nevertheless, I got on my knees for my evening prayer and began to rebuke that infirm spirit that was trying to attach itself to me. As I began to pray fervently, I actually felt that spirit of infirmity lift right up off of me as if something had

The Power of Declaration and Decrees

been resting upon my shoulders. What a revelation! If I hadn't experienced it I wouldn't understand demonic oppression and how spirits oppress Christians but can't possess them by means of unlawful entry. Pray fervently! Pray with expectation! Expect results!

Chapter 8

The Cost of Disobedience
"Faith for Foolishness"

Well, I told you that I would speak on how we can obtain faith for the negative and how our disobedience can cost us tremendously. You know, faith works both ways, remember? It depends on what you put action to. Obedience, Submission Faith is key to prospering while walking with God. Isaiah 1:19, "If you be willing and obedient, you will eat of the good of the land." Obedience is better than any sacrificial offering (1 Sam. 15:22). We cannot bribe God and replace obedience with superficial actions, things that do not profit. Disobedience can cost way more than we could ever be able to pay and we can derail our course and cause major setbacks. Consider Adam and Eve in the garden and the result of mankind because of disobedience. Every baby born today is born in sin and shaped in iniquity (Ps. 51:5). Look at the world around us and consider all of the current problems we are having because man decided to go in his own pernicious way and not walk according to the standards God set before him. So many of the social programs created today would not exist if mankind would have adhered to the commandments, laws and instructions of God.

So, I'm in church one Sunday morning, it's the call for service to begin, where everyone comes up to the altar for opening prayer. We sing a hymn and one of the ministers prays. At the end of the prayer, as we turn to go back to our seats while greeting one another, with a friendly smile, one brother, while saying good morning to me, also comments, "I sure would love to take you to dinner." Sounds innocent enough right? Dinner? How could that hurt? I smiled back with a friendly gesture and immediately as I took a step forward, it was literally as if a big hand reached out and hit me in the chest to stop me from moving forward and I heard these words, "Wrong spirit." But noooooooo! It's just dinner and besides, he's at the altar, in church, surely he must be okay, he must be saved. I pushed past the hand that I later learned was Holy Ghost warning me and trying to protect me from harm. The gentlemen, that he is, Holy Ghost, allowed me to go in my own pernicious way and obtain consequences for lining myself up for foolishness.

Well, needless to say, by the time it was all over, dinner turned out to be way more than the fried chicken that he came to my house to cook. The devil almost used him to cook my goose. By the end of it all, my yielding to the desires to be admired had me out of the will of God, in fornication, uncomfortable around the saints and I was saddened to find out that this guy was using drugs too! Oh, how did I find out that he was using drugs, I'm glad you asked? When I realized that he had gone in my kitchen drawer and –as my 4th grade teacher would have said, "He had the crust and unmitigated gall" to steal my money! When I asked him about it, he had the audacity to become offended! Slapped me in the face and ran out the door. Wrong answer. Yup, you guessed it. I'll just end it by saying that there was a soda bottle conveniently lying in the gutter of one of the streets I was running behind him in and I scooped it up, and slung it at him aiming directly at his head and only the Lord knows, how he just happened to be in 'slip and fall' mode as the bottle went sailing pass

The Cost of Disobedience

his head. Well, that was a lesson well learned, and a bitter pill to swallow. I had to go back to church with my head hung down but there was a suit and some of his other belongings in the trash dumpster and an end to what never should have started in the first place. Isaiah 1:19 & 20 baby! Better listen! Everyone is not guaranteed the same measure of grace and I'm sure there are plenty who would say today (I wish I didn't), *"Don't do it!"* We all know someone who did some of the same mess we did in the same era and they aren't here to tell about it OR they are still here but are telling the story with some different results. Uh-humm. That should have been me, it could have been me, it would have been me, if it wasn't for the Lord! So listen and use the tool of testimony of those who would dare share their experiences to help you. I often told my children when they were growing up, "Since I know where all of the holes are, I'm telling you so you don't have to fall in them. You can jump over them and have a headstart."

"Lord, thank you for your faithfulness to us. Help us to listen and to be obedient, so that our disobedience does not cause others to stumble or hinder ourselves from embracing our destiny."

Remember Lazarus, filled with sores and no earthly luxuries, who begged for the rich man's crumbs, died and was escorted into the bosom of Abraham? The rich man, however, who faired sumptuously with many goods in his lifetime died also and found himself in a place of torment begging for mercy and for Lazarus to be allowed to dip his finger in water and come and cool his tongue. After being denied, verse 27 states: "Then he said, I pray thee therefore, father, that thou wouldest send him to my father's house." In other words, "Since you denied my request and there is a great gulf between us, and he can't bring me water, can you at least send him to my father's house to warn my brothers so they can get it right because I definitely don't want them to come here! If it's anything I can do to stop that, please hear my cry!" Verse 28 says, "For I have five brethren; that he may testify unto them, lest they also come into this place of torment." This is the awesome part, verses 29-31, where Abraham answers, "They have Moses and the prophets, let them hear them. And he said, Nay, father Abraham: but if one went unto them from the dead, they will repent. And he said unto him, If they hear not Moses and the prophets, neither will they be persuaded though one rose from the dead." Amazing! Sounds like what's going on today; typical, human nature. The 'ole, *"I'm from Missouri- The Show Me State" mentality* Preachers are preaching the Word of God with power and conviction, it is packed with testimonies of the patriarchs, disciples and the red letter parables of Jesus himself. The Word that comes to make us wise unto salvation (2 Tim.3:15). The engrafted Word that is able to save our mortal souls (Jer.30:21). And we know that we overcome by the blood of the Lamb and the word of our testimony (Rev. 12:11). Then why is it so hard for people to believe, accept practical wisdom and receive instruction from the *'way-pavers'* if you will? Why do we have to have someone come back from the dead to tell us that there is a real hell? How do we have such a strong desire to jump in the holes anyway after someone shows us where each and every single one is (especially our young people with the alarming statistics of incarceration, homicide, teen pregnancy, and high percentage of AIDS amongst African American females)? It's amazing how we disregard wisdom. I'm concerned that the church doesn't have an ear to hear what the Spirit is saying if we can't even hear the man next door. I'm concerned that the young

The Cost of Disobedience

especially, don't have discernment and that the aged aren't as the sons of Issachar knowing the signs of the times. What if that bottle I threw had hit him? It could have been a very bad outcome for both of us, all due to *my* disobedience, not his. God spoke to *me* and I was the responsible party. It's so easy for us to want to blame the enemy for our fires when many times we are the arsonist. You know, the devil has your little black book and he will arrange, position, construct, organize, tempt, ensnare, plot, plan, scheme and just walk around seeking whom he may devour (1 Peter 5:8). Just because he sets the traps doesn't mean we have to walk into them. Just because he dials your number, doesn't mean you have to answer. Get a new ringtone.

In this hour we must hear what the Spirit is saying and we must obey. Jesus told the disciples to let their nets down on the other side of the boat after they toiled all night and caught nothing. Out of their obedience, they caught so many fish that the nets couldn't hold them. He also commanded the disciples to sit the people down after they followed Him, even though it appeared not to be enough food to feed them. After their obedience and everyone was fed with the five loaves and two fish, there was still food left over (Matt.14:17). See, that's why we must walk by faith and not by sight because we cannot believe everything we see (2 Cor. 5:7) for the "JUST SHALL LIVE BY FAITH" (Habakkuk 2:4, Rom1:17, Gal 3:11, Heb. 10:38).

The book of James opens the understanding of faith even greater by teaching us about the testing of faith and the prayer of faith. Chapter 2 verse 17 helps us to understand *dead faith*, and in verse 18 *working faith*, verse 19 *demonic faith* because it states that even the demons believe and tremble. Verse 22 shows an example of *perfected faith* and finally, verse 23 shows *rewarding faith* because Abra-

Let Faith Do It!

ham was called a "friend of God" after imputation of righteousness. Where is your faith?

Chapter 9

The Thing I Feared the Most Has Come Upon Me

We all have that one thing in the back of our mind (some may have more); the thing that brings concern and fear of how we will handle that specific encounter or be affected by it, if it shows up in our lives. We've heard heart-wrenching stories and have supported friends as well as family members who have faced some of life's trials and hard storms.

Job said, after receiving bad news about his sons and daughters, servants, oxen and camels and sickness that attacked his body, *"For the thing which I greatly feared is come upon me, and that which I was afraid of is come unto me"* (Job 3:25).

We know the story, Job was a man who made preparation everyday to worship and offer burnt offerings to God in case his sons had sinned and cursed God in their hearts. Thus did Job continually yet, in spite of his offerings, reverence for God and commitment to eschew evil by living a life that honored God, he still had a storm show up at his front door. This storm had a name *"the thing that Job feared."* There is a definite distinction between the two Hebrew words for FEAR that Job used. *"Yaré"* which means *"reverence"* indicates that Job showed high regard and respect for God and *"Puchad"* mean – *startled, afraid, alarmed, made to shake.* So somewhere in the midst of sacrifices, he had an agitation caused by expectation or realization of danger (Webster) that accompanied his reverence. His statements, *"greatly feared, and afraid of"* lets us know that in all of our attempts to operate in faith, fear can be operating somewhere. Fear is the enemy of faith and faith's opposite. It is *False Evidence Appearing Real*. Fear and Faith cannot occupy the same space. It's either one or the other. I'm not saying Job encountered a storm because he had fear. The story is clear, Satan was walking about and petitioned God for a time to test Job to prove that Job only served Him for the things he possessed. I'm just making a theological observation based upon his statement and reinforcing the fact that today as a New Testament believer, with a greater understanding of faith, and having the indwelling of the Holy Spirit, which they did not have of old, we have to walk in total faith, leaving no space for the entrance of fear. We cannot afford to allow fear to rent space. Give no space! Give no place!

    The difficulty of encountering a storm of this kind is in the fact that you feel like you've done everything right and you cannot justify the storm's significance based upon your right standing with God. Our sentiments would be, "How did this happen? How did the devil get in the door? I'm living a consecrated life, I'm prayed up. I have no active sin in my life." But we can think we're operating in faith and fear can be onboard. Job had a fear. In all of his sacrificing burnt offerings to God somewhere in his daily thoughts were "what if?" I'm just saying. *Now*, what happens is the enemy begins to work on your faith because his plan is to stop you from operating in it and become subjected to that what you can't explain. *"As a man thinks in his heart, so is he"* (Proverbs 23:7).

    I heard a profound man of God say that Sovereign Storms come to raise our trust to another level. They come to challenge the believer. That God uses these storms for the purpose of having a justifiable right to multiply, reward and bless us, like Job. Your promotion comes once you've passed the test. Oh! Did I say test? When you trust God your storm is just a test, regardless of its origin. Job was being tested by God and being set up even though it looked like a setback. Sometimes we are tested and I often tell people that everything isn't always the devil and in spite of the many faith terminologies and definitions, because there's Saving Faith, the faith it takes to receive salvation, Surrogate Faith, the faith used on the behalf of another, Submission Faith, just plain obedient "I believe God" Faith and so many more, that we've talked about but Jesus said it like this, *"If you have faith the grain of a mustard seed you can say to this mountain, Remove hence to yonder place; and it shall remove; and nothing shall be impossible unto you"* (Matt. 17:20).

One day, during prayer time, I heard the word, "Euroclydon" and not many days after, I heard my husband praying in his a.m. prayer and in his prayer tongue he said the same. It wasn't long after that that a storm hit our family. I will say to you that I experienced a season for about three years where I was being constantly challenged in character and faith while believing God for my covenant blessings, being engaged in constant spiritual warfare. I understood Jeremiah very well, yeah, it's shut up in my bones but I'm so worn out from the warfare that I don't have anything left. I can't talk about it. I remember telling my husband, "I feel like we have almost lost everything." Everything was under attack. But by this, we knew that God was making a divine announcement that our faith was under scrutiny like Job and we were about to LIVE! Live the abundant life that Christ promised and died for. We were a living epistle being read of men, faith being tried in the fire and to think it not strange, after we have suffered a while. I knew we were being settled, 'stablished and made perfect (mature) (1 Peter 5:10). We're about to reign with Him. Of course! A faith that cannot be tested is a faith that cannot be trusted! Paul says, "I'm going through this stuff for the furtherance of the Gospel and for your good" (Philippians 1:12). So in that season, we lost personal property my anniversary present that my husband bought me which was a Lexus automobile when a cab driver ran straight through a stop sign and totaled it. He didn't even get out and see if I was alright. I was hurt and I didn't believe the 2½ year lawsuit and compensation was comparable to the inconvenience and the injury. We lost a storage bin with many of our tools for our construction company, personal and ministry items. My husband accidentally threw away all of my ministerial ordination papers and degree documentation while cleaning the basement one day. That one I really took personal -- all of my hard work and accomplishments, excelling in ministry, studying to show myself approved! I felt like the devil sucker punched me right in the eye. Our children under attack, marriage under attack, and mom battling after a lengthy illness until she finally went home to be with the Lord. You know everybody that comes to church doesn't really have their mind focused on Jesus. Some folks' focus is off. They have ulterior motives, uhmm humm. Takes great men and women of God to discern and deal with accordingly. That devil will use circumstances and wait on you too. He'll wait right until the right test comes and you're right in the midst of a *"Jeremiah Syndrome"* to see if he can resurrect your old nature or discourage you or get a reaction and a show, so he can scar your testimony. But your scars can be turned into stars. Your story becomes your glory and the devil is a liar all the day long.

The Thing I Feared the Most Has Come Upon Me

He will build and build upon your pain, dismay, doubt & uncertainty until he feels like you're down enough for him to pounce upon! Remember, he seeketh whom he may devour. Then, finally my mother passed away in '08 after a lengthy illness. I thank God that I was able to obtain duplicate documentations with Doc. H. Jameson's original signature before he went home to glory and I'm grateful for the time spent with mom and hearing her say how proud she was of us. My husband and I share the testimony of the morning we left 6:00 a.m. prayer at our church to go to mom's house (led of the Spirit) to pray with her. What a move of God! All I will tell you is that at the end of the prayer, mom was speaking in tongues, caught up in the Holy Ghost and saying to us, "This is what God wanted all the time."

After my husband made a decision to transfer the ministry to California in 2007, we encountered the attack of emotional warfare, feelings of lost and discouragement because some of our family, friends and church members were saddened that we were leaving. At the time of the real estate decline, like everyone else, we felt the crunch. We were at the end our three year lease for the particular building that housed our church and Life Center and the owner's price increased to what we felt was way too unreasonable for the property (or our pocket). We had no mind to stress the membership out for a million dollar mortgage and we opted not to buy, so my husband closed the church. Well, he didn't actually close the church. He offered the option to area pastors who could benefit from a building of that magnitude who were probably in a better financial position to negotiate and we transferred our members (those who desired to stay) with a particular ministry. If you know anything about my husband, he is a "mover and a shaker" and as an entrepreneur, he has always been able to negotiate buildings. He has been instrumental in helping area pastors build churches as well.

While reading my word, I found out that *Euroclydon* simply means "a strong wind" (Acts 27:14). We serve a God that even the winds obey, so victory was always on my mind. However, there are just some things you don't like to hear Holy Spirit say. Ever try to change the meaning of the prophetic utterance that's coming out of your mouth because you don't want to hear it? There are certain words God uses to relay certain messages to me that usually mean that He is preparing me for something and I may need to be alert and aware. Aren't you glad we serve a God who speaks to the winds and the waves and tells them Peace Be Still! Thus, ours is not to worry and ours is not to fret, 'cause when you are anchored in Jesus what you see isn't necessarily what you're going to get.

I'm reminded of a day when I was traveling for my job and suddenly a torrential downpour came as I was driving down the road, so much so 'til I thought I might have to pull over. You know the kind - windshield wipers moving at rapid speed to what appears to be to no avail because a sheet of silver glazed water is laying on your windshield, and you're now treading through water and have been forced to move slowly through it when suddenly I crossed over one street and the storm was no more. Having this surreal moment, I looked through the rear view mirror and the storm was behind me still heavily pouring, but I had crossed over into an area where the storm ceased to be, just like that. Of course I looked up the scientific explanation for this on Wikipedia. I googled it too y'all, and the answer was simple. Most things have a beginning and an end. Just as it has to start somewhere, it

The Thing I Feared the Most Has Come Upon Me

has to end somewhere too (NOAA - National Severe Storm Laboratory). So in my closing (Oh oh the preacher is coming out and the author is taking a seat); Douglas Miller said it like this, "Though the storms keep on raging in my life, my soul has been (I'm just a "has been" y'all) anchored in the Lord. The breakers may dash, I shall not sway because He holds me fast..." And another artist penned it, "I told the storm... move!" Isaiah 43:2 says, *"When thou passest through the waters, I will be with thee; and through the rivers, they shall not overflow thee; when thou walkest through the fire, thou shalt not be burned; neither shall the flame kindle upon thee."* And *Yea!* Even though, I walk through the valley of the shadow of death, it's just a shadow. And I will FEAR no evil for thou art with me. Let the church say, Amen.

Chapter 10

Align Your Faith
"A Faith Alignment"

We must always make sure that what we are believing God for is in alignment with His Word. Oftentimes prayers are made and people become discouraged when their requests are not answered like they thought they should be. We have to remember that God is not apart from His Word. He is holy and does not partake in sinful nature or darkness. He is neither subject nor responsible to respond to anything outside of His Word; NOR can He. Anything asked outside of His Word will not produce fruitful results. I'm talking to the saints now. We can produce and reproduce some things on our own. Like Abraham and Sarah, we can conjure up some Ishmael stuff. So, if we're looking for Power Production Anointing, it must be based upon God's Word, mixed with faith and aligned. We are wrapped up, tied up, tangled up in Him. 1 John 5:14-15 states, *"And this is the confidence that we have in Him, that if we ask anything according to His will, He heareth us, And if we know that He hear us, whatsoever we ask, we know that we have the petitions that we desired of Him."*

Our faith request must be aligned with the Word of God. So praying imprecatory prayers like David did... one example.... Psalms 35:5, 6, was his plea for rescue, *"Let them be as chaff before the wind: and let the angel of the Lord chase him: Let their way be dark and slippery: and let the angel of the Lord persecute them."* Now, okay, he was talking about his enemy, but what if a person without understanding made this request because the Sunday School Teacher asked them to sit down and stop disrupting the class? Wasted energy, wasted time, wasted prayer. God's not honoring that prayer request but you will get an answer. God's answers to prayer are Yes, No and Not Yet. Therefore, no one can ever say that God did not respond. He probably didn't send the answer they wanted but He sent one.

This leads me to the final testimony. Most people who know me closely have heard the stories of the various attacks that I encountered via vehicle accidents. Nothing major, major, but just enough to do some aggravating damage. Thank God for His mercies and His covenant grace. Amazing, I thought at one point, "Maybe I should stay off the road; like, did I have a tag on my bumper that said 'Hi Hit Me?'" Yes, it was the negligence of a few drivers who rear ended me; once driving alone, once with my son in the car, and another as I was a front seat passenger headed to minister with our singing group. I was hit on my side of the passenger door while I was in the front seat in my sister's car. Her car was totaled and a taxi driver ran the stop sign and totaled the car my husband had just bought me for our anniversary. All this happened within a six year time period. So, I saw it as a mere instrument of the adversary's diabolical plot to attempt to wear me out, work on my patience and slow me down physically and discourage me right at the precipice of destiny. He obviously peeked into my future and saw what was coming. Not God inspired but God allowed. God does not "put sickness on us to teach us a lesson," which is a lie that has been taught for too long! Even in Job's test it was never God who placed the boils on him, it was Satan and God told him then how far he could go even with that test. Nevertheless, God intends to get the glory out of our test and we get the elevation.

So in one of those accidents I sustained a knee injury. I had all of the test, therapy, x-rays, *yada yada*. I was praying about the matter and consulting legal counsel at the same time. The Orthopedic Specialist diagnosed the need for arthroscopic surgery to fix the ligament that was torn. I wasn't entertaining that thought for one moment. Rather, I stood on what I knew about God's healing power and kept praying about it because it really did bother me more often than not and something needed to be done. Well, my husband and I, along with two other couples traveled to a Kenneth Copeland Meeting in Virginia and right in one of the worship services with my hands lifted high, I heard these words (now first let me prepare you because everyone cannot comprehend conversing with God on these levels and people feel like something is strange or questionable); if I can remember, this is what I heard (and I may be paraphrasing because it's been a long time since) - "I'm going to heal you but if I heal you now, you will be telling a lie at the court hearing, because you'll have to say your knee is injured in order to receive compensation for your pain and suffering from your lawsuit. I am going to heal you afterwards." It blew me away! He was right! At the deposition hearing, if they ask me if my knee is injured and God healed it, the answer would be no! I'd have no case and since the case was underway (and I guess God knew I could use *'dem dollaz*) He couldn't be a part of any darkness and He didn't want me to be either.

Well, you know the story, one day, somehow, after the case, I don't know when and I don't know where, but all I know is I looked down and realized that my knee wasn't hurting and I couldn't remember when it troubled

Let Faith Do It!

me last. God had healed the knee just like He said and I haven't had any problems with it ever again.

So sometimes what we're asking isn't in agreement with what God is doing or what He has already said. We need to take a look at some of our prayers and see if they are lining up with the word.

Chapter 11

So Very God!

This chapter talks about how God is concerned about even the little things that matter to us, how His love is greater than our Sunday morning experience and how He desires to be closer to us than I think we sometimes imagine. The story of Enoch was canonized for our enlightenment and to empower us to know that there is a reality in walking with God in such a spiritual dimension. Some may seem to think this kind of talk and/or expression of relationship with God is "off the deep end" and there have been many a critic regarding. We must remember that Adam was created for the purpose of fellowshipping with God, who came to fellowship with him in the evening regularly. There is the place where He reveals His secrets to those He can trust. There will be times when you will be misunderstood because of your recent conversation with the Almighty. There are those who can say. "No, I don't use an alarm clock. Holy Spirit awakens me. All I do is rely on Him and He knows the time I need to get up and He awakens me." So be it.

So Very God #1: One day, many years ago, as I was walking to work, very cold with limited finances, (as my baby days with God were all for my learning) I uttered out "Lord, I sure would like to have a cup of hot chocolate." Not very long after arriving to work and surely after forgetting all about it, one of my co-workers came to my office with a puzzled look on her face. This not really being strange to her because she herself being a believer, often witnessed the peculiar things that happen within the kingdom, asked me, "Do you like hot chocolate?" Stunned at her question I answered in hesitation "Ye-e-s-s, why?" She replied "Uh, because I feel like I'm supposed to bring you this hot chocolate." Smiling and rejoicing, I received the hot chocolate and told her the little story. I was so impressed with the love of God for that small moment in time and how He cared about a little cup of hot chocolate with all of the major concerns that the world had to be having that day. He really cared! Small as it may have been, it taught me a lot. I learned that He was closer than I ever imagined and that He heard everything I said and you can have what you ask for and you have to be mindful because you can also get what you say out of your mouth. It also taught me that God can and will use others to get your blessing to you AND walking with God and being sensitive to His voice is a special place to be.

So Very God #2: Raising the two girls (who were the only two born at the time), even though they were four years apart, we took pleasure in coordinating their outfits and dressing them alike. Well, one day a dear friend came to visit and as she often did, brought a box of clothing that her daughter could no longer fit for Kelli, the oldest daughter. Because she bought expensive clothing, this was always a blessing. In the box this time was also a beautiful full length rabbit coat and a green Rothchild one piece snowsuit. How nice! As time went on and it was nearing time to prepare to break out the winter gear, I thought, Humm…sure would like to get a nice fur coat for Terese to wear also. I'll have to see about where to get one." I can't tell you when, how long or especially now being some 20 plus years later… what? And I really don't remember discussing it. Because like I said, all I remember is that I had a "thought." Another friend, whom I hadn't seen in a while, called me one day, and after our conversation said, "Oh by the way, I have a few things that my daughter has outgrown and I'm sure they will fit Terese." "Cool! I'll stop by and get them, thanks" (I do have pictures). When I picked up the box of clothing, yup, you guessed it, a fur coat, same color, white, and this one was a jacket with the side pockets and a hood and oh…you thought I was finished, hold on! There was a two piece, green Rothchild snowsuit in the box too. So, very God! I am a witness that He will give you the desires of your heart, and He knows the intents of our hearts and hears our inward thoughts and before we have even prayed He has already sent the answer. He's that kind of friend, closer than a brother and just wants an opportunity to show Himself in our lives.

So Very God #3: One Saturday afternoon while preparing to do laundry, making errands in my jean skirt with kids in car, I'm suddenly led to make a detour and go pass my church to peak in on a youth service that was being held there by another visiting congregation. Once in the service, recognizing some of the mothers and enjoying the "Children of Light" choir with all that was going on in the service, near the end, someone asked me for remarks. Well, I didn't expect it, but suddenly without hesitation I stood on my feet and made this invitation, "Anyone who desires to be filled with the Holy Ghost, please come to the altar." Just as soon as I said it and as well as I heard it come out of my mouth, I immediately said to myself, "What in the world did I just say?! What did I just do?!" "whoo…." But it was too late to turn back now because when I looked at the altar it was full. Young people were making a decision for Christ and now it's "put up or shut up time." So in my "what you talking 'bout Willis" stroll down to the altar, with the "ool… I can't believe you did this to me" smirk, oozing out of my fixed smile, I came to the conclusion that, "Hey, I didn't say it so I'm not responsible for whatever is about to happen here." Well you know what happened? Because I released myself from the obligation of having to perform and placed the demand on the Holy Ghost, kids started receiving just like that. One girl just lifted her hands and before I could even touch her, she was speaking in tongues. Those children were so excited, they started dancing and praising God in that place! The mothers got excited and the fire was burning! Holy Ghost just needed a conduit, a means to reach them, a willing vessel. Someone who would get out of the way and let Him come in and do His work and I guess I was just prime for the picking that day or either young and naïve enough for Him to pick me out. Imagine how much we could accomplish in our services if we didn't have such tight, rigid programs and if we relied on Holy Spirit, allowing Him to speak and if we released ourselves from the obligations of having to perform and entertain people. If we would free ourselves from our own selfish agendas and one hour offering auctions, "who will give me a 10, 10, give me 5, 5" and flow in the spirit, it would be inevitable that we would encounter a move of God in our midst. I left that place amazed again. That was so very God! I had the day all planned out and He showed me that I was not my own, my footsteps were ordered, and He had a special assignment for me; the laundry could wait. I'm sure our plans must amuse God from time to time.

    I'm sure I can go on and on and each time I think I've ended, I think of something else to add to the book.

So Very God!

Let us pray: *Father God we thank you for your Word, your power and your love for us. It is your good pleasure to give us the kingdom and you have given us the keys to the kingdom that we might gain access and obtain every precious and exceeding promise and inheritance. Father, thank You for Your healing, covenant, grace, mercy and wrought work on Calvary's cross, for with Your stripes we are healed. You are our Deliverer, our Savior, our comfort and peace. Your Word teaches us, equips us and empowers us to walk by faith and not by sight. We have learned that all things are possible to him who believes. You have shown us by example throughout your Word that we can know You by divine intervention and that You are God of this whole universe. The earth is Yours, and You are the Lord thy God of all flesh and nothing is too hard for You. Father, thank you for understanding of Your Word and the power that lies within it for Your Word is quick, sharp and powerful, never changing, ever challenging, always true. Thank You for proverbial wisdom, poetry, history, correction, instruction and for the parables of Your son, Jesus. Thank You that we are living epistles written of men. Help us to trust You at new levels and testify of Your goodness to those who need hope. Our sole desire is to serve You and do Your perfect will and build Your kingdom, amen.*

The end

About the Author

Dr. Fields is a graduate of the International Christian University, Jameson School of Theology and Atlantic Community College. She is an Alumni Professor of Jameson School of Ministry and former student of Montclair State University. Dr. Fields is Co-Pastor of Greater Works Ministries, Inc., Conference Host and one of today's prophetic voices.

www.ingramcontent.com/pod-product-compliance
Lightning Source LLC
Chambersburg PA
CBHW032017290426
44109CB00013B/695